Horizon of the Unseen

Visual Reflections on Spiritual Themes

EDITED & ILLUSTRATED BY CORINNE RANDALL

intellect™
Bristol, UK
Portland, OR, USA

"Horizon of the Unseen"

Painting exists on the "Horizon of the Unseen". This is because it uses visual imagery to symbolize hidden spiritual meanings. There are two ways of looking at the world: One beholds everything as signs or traces leading from the diversity back to the oneness, the other sees only the apparent and obvious appearance. Painting unites these two ways of seeing because it is a physical act that requires a spiritual condition. Like the melody that comes in on the off beat of a rhythm, holding some elusive quality between these two moments, the tension between figurative and abstract forms can be used to express the mysterious beauty of this life.

This compilation of writings is taken from a wide spectrum of cultural traditions and presented within twelve categories. A holistic vision appears from which it is possible to bring out by contrast the essential characteristics of each theme. Art unites the dualities of the personal and the universal. These universal motifs therefore provide a framework that contains infinite possibilities for expression of the spiritual through art.

The quotes are taken from the following authors - Jalalu' d-Din Rumi (1207-1273 A.D.) and Mahamud Shabestan, Sufi poets (Islamic Tradition). Loy Ching Yuen and Lao Tzu from the Taoist tradition. Báha'u'lláh (1817-1892) and Abdu'l-Bahá (1844-1921) from the Bahá'i Faith, Moses de Leon, a 13th century Jewish cabalist, St. John of the cross, 16th century Christian mystic and Hindu scriptures. Political leaders - Nelson Mandella, Chief Seattle (Native American) and Marcus Aurelius (Roman Emperor). T.S.Eliot and Hellen Keller.

Contents

Spiritual Journey

The doors of the spiritual

kingdom are open to all.

ABDU'L-BAHA

Thou art but one step away

From the glorious heights above.

Take thou one pace and with the next

advance into the immortal realm.

BAHA'U'LLAH

The pathway of life is the road that leads

to divine knowledge and attainment.

ABDU'L-BAHA

Never loose hope if the beloved pushes you away.

It is your patience that will draw him back.

If he blocks all your roads, be sure.

He will show you a secret way unknown to others.

RUMI

When the heart is pure the spirit enters,

and our growth is natural and assured.

ABDU'L-BAHA

The way is unimpeded harmony;

Its potential may never be fully exploited.

It is as deep as the source of all things:

It blunts the edges, resolves the complications,

harmonizes the light.

LAO TZU

The wayfarer who journeyeth

unto the Crimson Pillar

in the snow-white path,

will never reach his heavenly goal

unless he abandoneth all

that men possess.

The wayfarer ascendeth unto a City

that hath no name or description,

and whereof one heareth neither sound nor mention.

Therein flow the oceans of eternity,

whilst the sun of the Unseen shineth resplendent

above the horizon of the Unseen.

BAHA'U'LLAH

We shall not cease from exploration

And the end of all our exploring

Will be to arrive where we started

And know the place for the first time.

T.S.ELIOT

LIGHT

Our deepest fear is not that we are inadequate. Our deepest fear is that we are powerful beyond measure. We are all meant to shine as children do and as we let our own light shine, we unconsciously give other people the permission to do the same.

NELSON MANDELA

Love is the light that guideth in darkness,

The living link that assureth the progress

of every illumined soul.

ABDU'L-BAHA

Every particle of the world is a mirror,

in each atom lies the blazing light of a thousand suns.

MAHAMUD SHABESTAN

The Reality of Divinity may be compared to the sun,

which from the height of its magnificence shines

upon all the horizons and each horizon,

and each soul, receives a share of its radiance.

If this light and these rays did not exist,

beings would not exist.

The rays of the Sun of Truth are shed upon all things

and shining within them,

and telling of that Day-Star's splendours,

Its mysteries, and the spreading of Its lights.

ABDU'L-BAHA

As the sun ripens the fruits of the earth and

gives life and warmth to all living beings,

so shines the Sun of Truth on all souls filling them

with the fire of Divine love and understanding.

ABDU'L-BAHA

Keep your face to the sunshine

and you cannot see the shadow.

HELLEN KELLER

The rays of the Sun of Reality

will be reflected in your heart.

INNER VISIONS

" Men should hold in their souls
the vision of celestial perfection,
and there prepare a dwelling-
place for the inexhaustible
bounty of the divine spirit."

Abdu'l-Baha

Leaf sounds talk together

like poets making fresh metaphors.

The green felt cover slips,

and we get a flash

of the mirror underneath.

RUMI

The visible world was made to correspond

to the world invisible and

there is nothing in this world but that which is a symbol

of something in that other world.

AL GHAZALI

Trees show the bodily form of the wind,

Waves give vital energy to the moon.

ZERIN KUSHU

Love is the unique power that bindeth together

the diverse elements of this material world,

the supreme magnetic force that directeth

the movements of the spheres in the celestial realms.

ABDU'L-BAHA

O Universe, all that is in tune with you

is also in tune with me!

Every note of your harmony

resonates in my innermost being.

MARCUS AURELIUS

In every leaf ineffable delights are treasured

and within every chamber

unnumbered mysteries lie hidden.

BAHA'U'LLAH

Sorrow not

for days of blissful joy, of heavenly delight,

are assuredly in store for you.

Worlds, holy and spiritually glorious,

will be unveiled before your eyes.

To each and every one of them you will no doubt attain.

BAHA'U'LLAH

Paradise

Have ye forgotten that true and

radiant morn, when in those

hallowed and blessed surroundings

ye were all gathered

beneath the shade of the tree of life,

which is planted in

the all-glorious paradise?

BAHA'U'LLAH

Flight

How could the soul not take flight

when from the glorious Presence

a soft call flows sweet as honey,

comes right up to her and whispers,

"Rise up now, come away."

RUMI

Cast away that which ye possess,

and, on the wings of detachment,

soar beyond all created things.

BAHA'U'LLAH

Break all fetters and seek for

spiritual joy and enlightenment;

Then, though you walk on this earth,

You will perceive yourselves

to be within the divine horizon.

ABDU'L-BAHA

Our body is like a cage and the spirit is like a bird.

If the cage becomes broken the bird will continue to exist.

The bird of her soul escaped! Free of the body and the grieving,

flying in a vast simple region that was itself, where it could sing its truth!

RUMI

Freedom is not a matter of place,

but of condition.

If we are imprisoned in the material world,

our spirit can soar into the Heavens

and we shall be free indeed.

ABDU'L-BAHA

The Ocean

This most great,

this fathomless and surging

ocean is near,

astonishingly near,

unto you.

Behold it is closer to you

than your life-vein!

BAHA'U'LLAH

Look not at your own capacities,

for the divine bestowal can transform

a drop into an ocean.

ABDU'L-BAHA

Your souls are as waves on the sea of the spirit;

although each individual is a distinct wave,

the ocean is one, all are united.

ABDU'L-BAHA

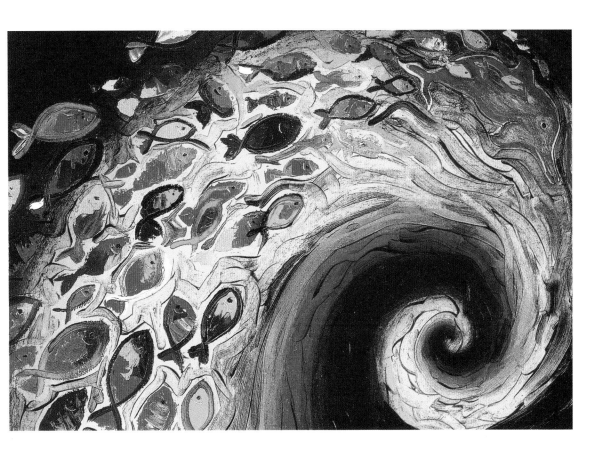

Divine bestowals are like the sea

and we are like the fishes in that sea.

The fishes must not look at themselves;

They must behold the ocean which is vast and wonderful.

Provision for the sustenance of all is in this ocean.

ABDU'L-BAHA

O Lord! O Thou Whose bounty granteth wishes!

I stand before Thee, all save Thee forgetting.

Grant that the mote of knowledge in my Spirit

Escape desire and the lowly clay;

Grant that Thine ancient gift, this drop of wisdom,

Merge with Thy mighty sea.

RUMI

Transcending Suffering

> Whatsoever may happen is for the best, because affliction is but the essence of bounty, and sorrow and toil are mercy unalloyed, and anguish is peace of mind, and to make a sacrifice is to receive a gift.
>
> ABDU'L-BAHA

When something unique becomes many, it looses its value.

Yet many are the sorrows of the heart but they become precious gems

on the path to the beloved.

RUMI

Don't worry about saving these songs.

And if one of our instruments breaks,

it doesn't matter.

We have fallen into the place

where everything is music.

RUMI

Like a golden beacon signaling
on a moonless night,
Tao guides our passage
through this transitory realm.
In moments of darkness and pain
remember all is cyclical.
Sit quietly behind your wooden door:
Spring will come again.

LOY CHING YUEN

Happiness

Life is created for happiness

All the sorrow and the grief that exist

come from the world of matter.

The spiritual world bestows only joy.

ABDU'L-BAHA

Man is, in reality, a spiritual being,
and only when he lives in the spirit
is he truly happy.

ABDU'L-BAHA

Peace

When a man surrenders all desires that come to the heart then his soul has indeed found peace.
HINDU SCRIPTURES

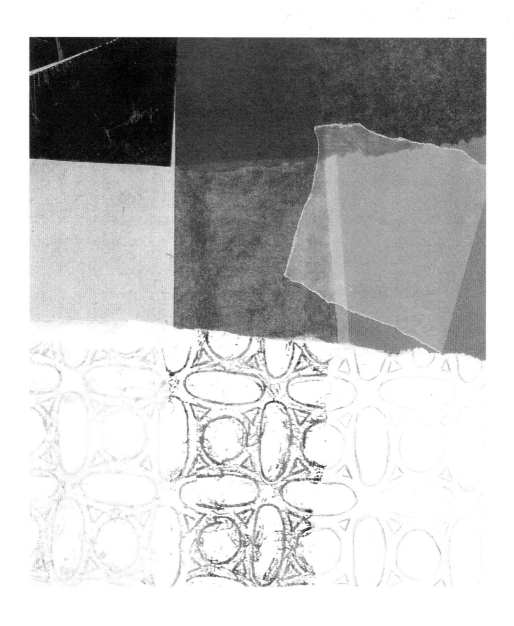

When a thought of war comes,

oppose it by a stronger thought of peace.

A thought of hatred must be destroyed

by a more powerful thought of love.

ABDU'L-BAHA

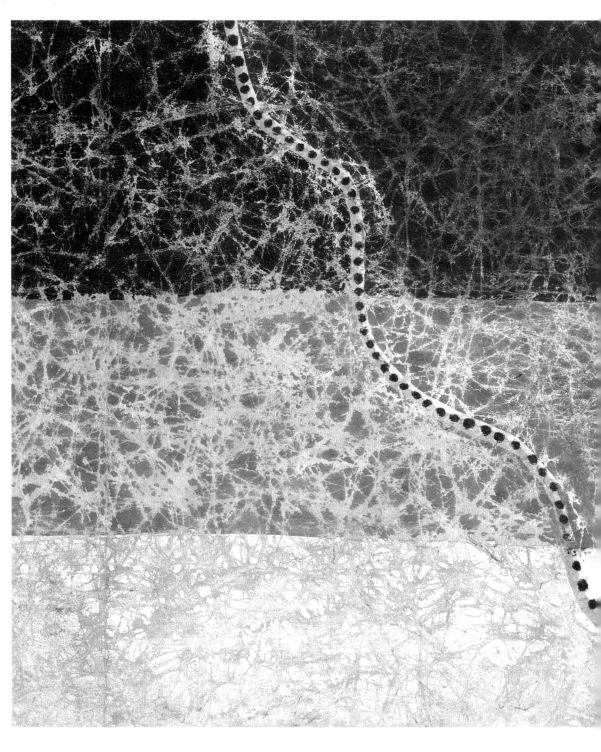

I can hear the silence any time I remember to listen.

It's right below the noise.

PENNY PEIRCE

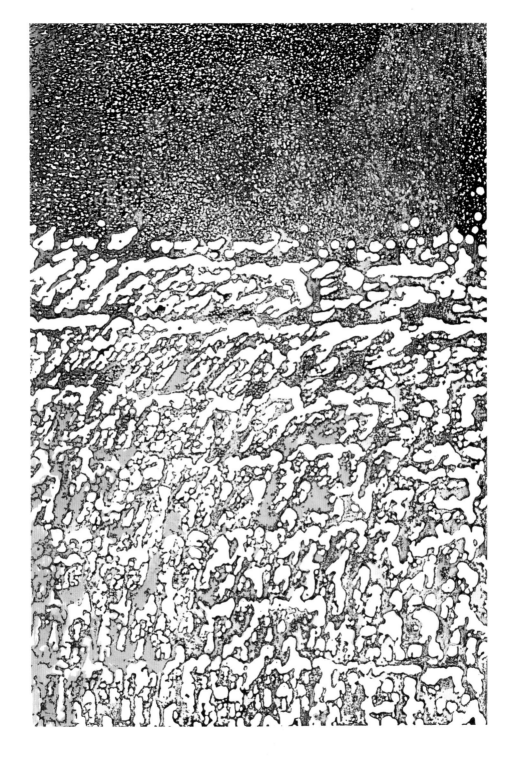

Let thine everlasting melodies breathe tranquillity upon me.

BAHA'U'LLAH

RELIGIONS ARE MANY,
BUT THE REALITY
OF RELIGION IS

ONE

The entire chain is one.
Down to the last link, everything
is linked with everything else;
so divine essence is below as
well as above, in heaven and
on earth. There is nothing else.

MOSES DE LEON

Whoever sees all beings in himself
And himself in all beings   Does not,
By virtue of such realization,   hate
anyone.   When all beings are realized
As existing in his own self,   then what
Illusion, what sorrow, can afflict him,
Perceving as he does the   Unity ?

HINDU SCRIPTURE

If a dove from the East and a dove from the West, a dove from the North and a dove from the South to at the chance arrive, same

time, in one spot, they immediately associate in harmony.

ABDU'L-BAHA

Do not look at the shortcomings of anybody; see with the sight of forgiveness. The imperfect eye beholds *imperfections.*

ABDU'L-BAHA

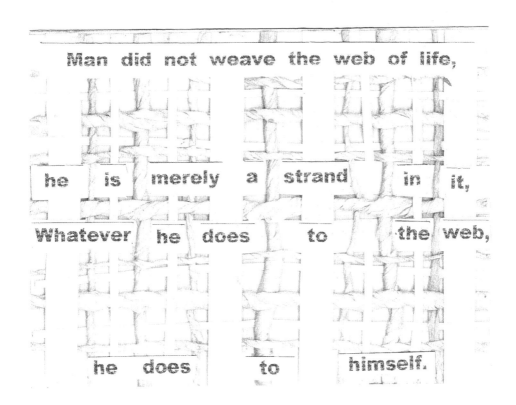

Man did not weave the web of life,

he is merely a strand in it,

Whatever he does to the web,

he does to himself.

CHIEF SEATTLE

The Soul

As great as the infinite space beyond

is the space within the lotus of the heart.

Both heaven and earth are contained

in that inner space, both fire and air,

sun and moon, lightning and stars.

CHANDOGYA UPANISHAD

The Soul is of one indivisible substance and therefore eternal. The Soul is of one indivisible substance and therefore eternal. The Soul is of one indivisible substance and therefore eternal. The Soul is of one indivisible substance and therefore eternal.

Nothingness

That you may have pleasure in everything,

Seek your pleasure in nothing.

That you may know everything,

Seek to know nothing.

That you may possess all things,

Seek to possess nothing.

That you may be everything,

Seek to be nothing.

ST. JOHN OF THE CROSS

The greatest thing seems incomplete

yet it never wears out.

The fullest thing seems empty

yet it never runs dry.

TAO TE CHING

Try and be a sheet of paper

with nothing on it.

Be a spot of ground

where nothing is growing,

where something might be planted,

a seed, possibly, from the absolute.

RUMI

Guided meditation sessions on the themes covered in this book are held Wednesdays 7.30pm at Akousis, 1, Fairlawn Rd. Montpelior, Bristol. To confirm dates please telephone Corinne on 0117 9413247

REFERENCES

p.4   Abdu'l-Baha, *Japan will turn ablaze: Writings of Abdu'l-Baha*, Shoggi Effendi

p.5   Baha'u'llah, *The Hidden Words.* No.4 from the Persian, Wilmette Publishing Trust

p.6   Abdu'l-Baha, *Foundations*, p.78 / Rumi, *Hidden Music*, Maryam Mafi, p.80. Thorsons 2001.

p.7   Abdu'l-Baha (source unknown) / Lao Tzu, *Tao Te Ching*; (*Essential Mystics*, Andrew Harvey 1996, Castle Books, p.19)

p.8   Baha'u'llah, *The Seven Valleys and The Four Valleys* p.58 (Wilmette Publishing Trust, 1991)

p.9   Baha'u'llah, *Gems of Divine Mysteries.* 114 (Baha'i World Centre 2002) / T.S.Eliot, *Little Gidding.*

p.10   Nelson Mandela

p.11   Abdu'l-Baha, Some Answered Questions, pp. 221-222 / Mahamud Shabestan.

p.12   Abdu'l-Baha, p.41 *Selections*

p.13   Abdu'l-Baha, *Paris Talks*, p.27

p.14   Abdu'l-Baha, *Selections* p.203

p.15   Hellen Keller /Abdu'l-Baha, Adapted from *Some Answered Questions* p.206 Baha'i publishing trust , Wilmette 1990

p.16   Abdu'l-Baha, *Paris Talks.* p.99

p.17   Rumi,*The Essential Rumi,* Coleman Barks. Penguin. 1995 p.146.

p.18   Al Ghazali, Margaret Smith, *The Mystic* (London: Luzac and Company, 1944) / From the Zerin Kushu, in Watts, p.139

p.19   Abdu'l-Baha, *Selections*, p.27

p.20   Marcus Aurelius, from *Meditations.* (*Essential Mystics* p.135, Andrew Harvey) / Baha'u'llah, *Book of certitude*, p.198

p.21   Baha'u'llah, *Gleanings* p.329 (Wilmette publishing Trust 1994)

p.22   Baha'u'llah, *Hidden Words* 19 Persian.

p.25   Rumi, p.157 *Essential Mystics*

p.26   Baha'u'llah, *Gleanings* p. 319

p.27   Abdu'l-Baha, *Abdu'l-Baha in London.* p.87. (London: Baha'i Publishing Trust, 1982)

p.28   Abdu'l-Baha, *Some Answered Questions* p.228 (Wilmette,Illinois publishing Trust 1964) / Rumi, Hidden Music p.118

p.29   Abdu'l-Baha, *Paris Talks*, pp.111

p.30   Baha'u'llah, *Baha'i World Faith*, p.67

p.32   Abdu'l-Baha, *The Promulgation of Universal Peace*, p.131

p.33   Abdu'l-Baha, *Paris Talks* pp. 83-84

p.34   Abdu'l-Baha, *Paris Talks* pp. 83-84

p.35   Rumi, *The Mathavi* (p. 57 *The Seven Valleys*, Baha'i Publishing Trust, Wilmette, Illinois, 1945)

p.36   Abdu'l-Baha, *Selections* p.26 (Baha'i World Centre 1982)

p.37   Rumi, *Hidden music.* P.139

p.38   Rumi, *The Essential Rumi*, Coleman Barks. Penguin Books 1999 p.34

p.40   Loy Ching Yuen - Taoist tradition. p.33 *Essential Mystics* (Andrew Harvey, Castle Books 1996)

p.43   Abdu'l-Baha, *The Divine Art of Living*, p.18

p.44   Abdu'l-Baha, *Paris Talks*, 35:1, 3, p.110 (1995)

p.45   Abdu'l-Baha, *Paris Talks* 23:7 p.68 (1995)

p.48   Hindu Scriptures, *The Bhagavad Gita* (*The Peace Bible*, pp.22-23)

p.49   Abdu'l-Baha, *Paris Talks*, p.29 (Baha'i Publishing Trust 1979)

p.50   Penny Peirce, *Intuition.* p.92 Beyond Words Publishing Inc 1997

p.51   Baha'u'llah , *Remembrance of God.* No. 83 p.90 Baha'i Publishing Trust. Wilmette 1945

p.52   Abdu'l-Baha, *The Promulgation of Universal Peace.* pp. 126-129

p.53   Moses de Leon, Jewish Tradition.p.103 *Essential Mystics* (Illustration by Max Morris)

p.54   *Isa Upanishads*, Hindu Scripture. (p.100, *The Peace Bible*) Abdu'l-Baha

p.55   Abdu'l-Baha, *The Promulgation of Universal Peace.* p. 93/
Chief Seattle (p.36 Brendan O'Malley, *God at every Gate*, Canterbury Press, Norwich 1997)

p.56   *Chandogya Upanishad* – Hindu Scriptures

p.57   Abdu'l-Baha, *Paris Talks* pp. 90-91 (1979, Baha'i Publishing Trust, London)

p.58   St. John of the Cross. p11 *Lamps of Fire.* Elizabeth ODC Darton. Longman and Todd 1985.

p.59   Tao Te Ching – *Parabola* p79 1996 *Peace.*

p.62   Rumi, *The Essential Rumi,* Back cover.

First Published in the UK in 2005 by
Intellect Books, PO Box 862, Bristol BS99 1DE, UK

First Published in the USA in 2005 by
Intellect Books, ISBS, 920 NE 58th Ave. Suite 300, Portland, Oregon 97213-3786, USA

A catalogue record for this book is available from the British Library

ISBN 1-84150-913-2

Publisher: Masoud Yazdani
Book Design: Corinne Randall

Printed and bound in Great Britain by Orchard Press